THE MORINI STRAD

Willy Holtzman

BROADWAY PLAY PUBLISHING INC
New York
www.broadwayplaypublishing.com
info@broadwayplaypublishing.com

THE MORINI STRAD
© Copyright 2013 Willy Holtzman

Cover photo by Robert Curtis
First edition: February 2013
I S B N: 978-0-88145-560-1
Book design: Marie Donovan
Page make-up: Adobe InDesign
Typeface: Palatino
Printed and bound in the U S A

THE MORINI STRAD was developed at PlayPenn (Paul Meshijian, artistic director), and at Perry-Mansfield (Andrew Leynse, artistic director).

THE MORINI STRAD premiered at City Theatre in Pittsburgh, PA on 6 November 2010. The cast and creative contributors were:

ERICA ....Carla Belver
BRIAN..David Whalen

Director.. Daniella Topol
Set design... Tony Ferrieri
Costume design..Angela M Vesco
Lighting design ....Dennis Parichy
Sound design.. Brad Peterson
Original musical composition........................... Louise Beach
Production stage manager .... Patti Kelly

THE MORINI STRAD had its New York premiere at Primary Stages on April 3, 2012. The cast and contributors were:

ERICA .... Mary Beth Peil
BRIAN .... Michael Laurence
VIOLINIST .... Hanah Stuart

Director .... Casey Childs
Set design .... Neil Patel
Costume design .... David C Woolard
Lighting design .... M L Geiger
Sound design .... Lindsay Jones
Projection designer .... Jan Harley
Music consultant .... Louise Beach
Production stage manager .... Sarah Melissa Hall

CHARACTERS & SETTING

BRIAN, *40s*
ERICA, *70s/80s*

Time: The recent past

Place: Upper Fifth Avenue Manhattan and a near suburb

Prologue

(A once-elegant upper Fifth Avenue apartment. The furnishings have not been replaced in decades. Even the light through the curtained windows seems somehow old.)

(ERICA MORINI, a woman of advanced if indeterminate years, suffers noticeably as an unseen student violinist labors through the third movement of the Bruch Violin Concerto No. 1.)

ERICA: Thank you, please. That's quite enough. No more. I beg you, no more.

(The music stops.)

ERICA: Well, that certainly was very athletic, my young friend. You must be quite exhausted. Perhaps your instrument is also somewhat exhausted.

(Up on BRIAN SKARSTAD's modest violin workshop. He works on a neck graft repair.)

BRIAN: When sixteen year-old violin prodigy Jascha Heifetz made his Carnegie Hall debut, another violinist turned to a pianist friend and said, "It's awfully hot in here." The friend grinned, "Not for pianists." That's a musician's idea of a joke. I'm a violin maker. The good thing about my line of work is that there are no prodigies. Children and sharp objects, bad combination. We are the un-prodigies of the music world. Now if we could only figure out a way to get by without violinists.

ERICA: Yes, the little finger is essential in the performance of the spiccato. But it is absolutely useless in all the detache strokes above the middle of the bow. Too much bouncing, too much percussion. There must be none of this *kratz*— How do you say this? "Scratch."

BRIAN: They don't know anything about the guts of a fiddle. A spruce top, for instance. *(Holds up two quarter cut pieces of spruce.)* Soft wood. Very hard to join the separate halves. The plane snags or chatters—kindling.

ERICA: This bowing technique of yours—it is good to be forceful, but one is not slicing salami. I exaggerate. But for your own good. To bow properly is not to force the music into the violin. Proper bowing releases the music that is already inside.

(BRIAN pings wood planks against each other.)

ERICA: Provided it is, indeed, inside.

BRIAN: *(Presses the spruce pieces together)* We're talking seamless. Like twins separated at birth, united again. Whole. Do violinists know this? Do they even care? They're too busy looking over their shoulder for the next prodigy. Violinists are a necessary evil. *(Glances at his watch—he's late for an appointment.)*

ERICA: Get a tissue, a drink of water.

BRIAN: *(Removing his apron)* But what do I know?

ERICA: Emotion is good.

BRIAN: I'm just an artisan.

(Slips on a worn sports jacket)

ERICA: I say these things for your own good.

BRIAN: Not an artist.

ERICA: Very well, then. Bowing. *(Reaching for a violin case)* Here, I will show you…

One

(ERICA's *apartment. The doorbell rings. And again. She waits for one more ring then opens the door on* BRIAN.)

ERICA: You're late, Mister Skarstad.

BRIAN: Forgive me, Ms Morini, but…

ERICA: *(Rapidly)* Mrs. Mister is departed, but that is hardly reason to neuter "Mrs" of its "r" having previously been abridged if not aborted from *maitresse*.

BRIAN: My apologies, Mrs Morini. I'm sorry you lost your husband.

ERICA: You make it sound as if I misplaced him. I know precisely where he is—under an elm tree at Cedar Park going on fifteen years. He was several years my senior. In any case, he was not Mister Morini. That was my father. Morini is a stage name, or rather a family name, or, it seems, custom dictates one says "maiden" name, though it's centuries since I was a maiden, and in any case, you are hardly here to absorb the sordid details of my deflowering.

BRIAN: I'm running a little late. And when no one came to the door…

ERICA: It's such an epic apartment. I'm at sixes and sevens whenever the staff is on leave.

BRIAN: Butler's day off?

ERICA: One wishes. I am reduced to nurse Dunham and a most disagreeable housekeeper, whose name escapes me. *(Beat)* Felice.

BRIAN: The nurse or the housekeeper?

ERICA: My husband. Do you always find names so confusing?

BRIAN: Not as a rule.

ERICA: Felice Siracusano. He was a diamond broker.

BRIAN: My Uncle Norm is a jeweler.

ERICA: Felice was not a "jeweler". He did not engrave bracelets. He was, as I said, in the diamond business.

(BRIAN *steps onto a faded Persian rug.* ERICA *glares at his shoes. He steps back onto the door mat and wipes his feet.*)

ERICA: It was Papa's Persian. Purchased in Persia. While I was performing. In Tehran.

(ERICA *motions for* BRIAN *to sit. He surveys the room and finds the least uncomfortable looking chair. It groans under his weight.*)

ERICA: Ball or bag?

BRIAN: I'm sorry?

ERICA: Tea bag or loose?

BRIAN: Please, don't bother.

ERICA: No bother, to speak of. Of course, the help is scarcely to be trusted. It's a wonder I still have a tea service at all. You look like Darjeeling to me.

BRIAN: Dar(*jeeling*).

ERICA: Black tea from the Himalayas. A thinking man's Lipton. But I don't suppose they distract you with such refinements as high tea at violin making school.

BRIAN: I did go to college, not that we had tea there, either.

ERICA: Perhaps I've heard of it.

BRIAN: Wesleyan.

ERICA: A Methodist school. Not exactly Yale, is it? No matter. Such hysterics about which decal one places on the window of one's automobile. I had no formal education beyond secondary school, and barely that. But I'm fluent in seven languages and I know one variety of tea from another. You trained in Italy, Germany, France?

BRIAN: Utah.

ERICA: From Methodists to Mormons. Is that where you became familiar with my work?

BRIAN: Violin making school? Uh, no.

ERICA: At college, of course. You had a better education than I imagined.

BRIAN: Not there either, really.

ERICA: When exactly did you first hear my name?

BRIAN: Yesterday, on your voice mail message.

(A tea kettle whistles offstage.)

ERICA: Darjeeling, then, Mister Skarstad?

BRIAN: Brian.

ERICA: *(Irritated)* Do call me Mrs Morini. *(Exits)*

BRIAN: *(Calling after)* The Prier School. Peter Prier. He's German. *(He stands and inspects the room, running his finger along the fringed lamp shade and the dusty leather-bound books.)*

ERICA: *(Offstage)* Pass auf!

BRIAN: I'm being "careful". I was wondering, how did you get my name?

ERICA: *(Offstage)* Was it the Yellow Pages?

BRIAN: I'm not in the book.

(ERICA returns straining under the weight of a silver tea service and a silver toast holder holding toast with the crust removed.)

BRIAN: Here, let me help you with that.

(BRIAN takes the tray from ERICA and carefully lowers it onto the coffee table.)

ERICA: How mysterious of you, having an unlisted phone number.

BRIAN: I'm not impossible to find, obviously. I'm selective. The thing is I work out of my house and I have children.

ERICA: One needn't boast of procreation.

BRIAN: I'm n(ot)...my family is very important to me.

ERICA: We all have our little indulgences, don't we? Did you bring the item I requested?

BRIAN: Item?

ERICA: Please. The toast is getting cold.

BRIAN: Oh, the jelly!

ERICA: *(All broad "a"s)* Marmalade.

BRIAN: I had to replay the message three times to realize you meant...marmalade. *(Removes a jar from his bag)* There.

ERICA: *(Disappointed)* Orange?

BRIAN: And there, and there. *(Removes two more jars)*

ERICA: Lime. Ginger! *(She strains at the jar lid but her hands are too arthritic to open it.)*

BRIAN: Those lids tend to stick.

(Opens a jar. ERICA meticulously spreads two slices of toast with marmalade. BRIAN pops a slice into his mouth.)

ERICA: Felice wouldn't let me near the kitchen. "We must protect those precious hands!" Whenever he was away on business I baked and baked. You couldn't get me out of that kitchen. I was known for my strudel. Since he died, I don't bake so much anymore. What were we talking about?

BRIAN: How...

ERICA: How I got your obnoxiously unlisted phone number from a member of the Kyoto Quartet whose name is virtually unpronounceable.

BRIAN: Haruki Nakamura. He's a friend of yours?

ERICA: I daresay he'd call himself a "disciple." So many do. He owns you, I believe.

BRIAN: I made a violin for him.

ERICA: An original Skarstad! Of course, I've only ever heard him perform on a Stradivarius.

BRIAN: I'm Haruki's back-up. Airplanes, altitude, climate—Strad didn't know his fiddles would be traveling so far beyond the Cremona city limits.

ERICA: Violinists only care about the all-consuming sound. We don't stop to think that it began with a chunk of wood.

BRIAN: Quarter-cut flamed maple. More of a wed(*ge*).

ERICA: What's that like for you?

BRIAN: Starting a violin? It's been a little while. What's it like? I don't know, exhilarating. Exacting. Maybe a little how a novelist feels staring at a blank page. No, a ream of blank pages. But with the first push of the arching gouge I can hear the music in the wood. And I see the violin.

ERICA: Were you to describe a Skarstad, what adjectives might come to mind?

BRIAN: No adjectives. It works.

ERICA: Like a chest of drawers.

BRIAN: Open one of those drawers with just the right touch and…who knows, maybe a little magic.

ERICA: Haruki said the instrument wasn't half-bad, once he played it in.

BRIAN: He said that?

ERICA: Words to that effect. Once one sorts out all the "r"s and "l"s the conversation is already miles down the road. He also mentioned you have a certain genius for repair.

BRIAN: That's how I pay the bills. And right now restorations add up to more than original Skarstads.

ERICA: There are originals, and there are "originals". Perhaps three or four centuries from now…

BRIAN: I'm just trying to get through the next month. So it's a restoration you have in mind?

ERICA: If you're up to it.

BRIAN: I can fix anything.

ERICA: One "fixes" an oversexed mutt.

BRIAN: Mend, heal, revive—whatever you want to call it. I'm your man. Invisible, like it never happened.

ERICA: Are all Utah luthiers so supremely confident?

BRIAN: I had my choice of schools. I chose Utah. I grew up there. I played viola in the Utah Youth Symphony.

ERICA: You needn't recite your curriculum vitae. I'm merely curious why would one apprentice Out West, given all the other options. Pierre Bouchier is just over on 57th Street.

BRIAN: Then why waste your time with me? By all means, call Pierre. Give him my regards. Tell him I don't regret turning down that job offer of his. *(He stands and crosses to the door.)*

ERICA: I did not give you permission to leave! I have concertized in all the great halls of Europe. I have performed before kings and queens. And I am not about to have a violin repairman walk out on me!

(BRIAN hesitates.)

ERICA: Besides, if you're half the luthier you claim to be, you will not leave without first seeing the particular instrument in need of repair. *(She crosses to the silver* closet. *She removes a skeleton key that hangs by a strand around her neck. She opens the closet door and with some effort lowers a battered violin case from the top shelf. She places the case on the table in front of* BRIAN.*)* You may open the case. But you must not touch what is inside until I say so.

*(*BRIAN *lifts the lid.)*

ERICA: It's under the silk scarf which, in case you're interested, was given me by Toscanini for my flawless unaccompanied Bach.

*(*BRIAN *removes the scarf. He gazes on the violin and fights to retain his Scandinavian reserve.)*

ERICA: Behold...

BRIAN & ERICA: ...the Davidoff Stradivarius!

(Overlapping, counterpointing)

BRIAN: Holy shit!

(On a nod from ERICA, BRIAN *lovingly lifts the violin and examines it sideways across the arch.)*

BRIAN: Look at the tool marks on the scroll, the chamfer is still black...

ERICA: *(Drapes the scarf over her shoulders)* Arturo was a most charming man. I have a weakness for Italian men.

BRIAN: The purfling mitres are long and graceful—just like the Dupont Strad.

ERICA: Arturo absolutely detested Mussolini. In 1931 at Teatro Comunale Arturo refused to perform the fascist anthem.

BRIAN: It's still covered with the original Cremonese varnish. And the maple back—I know that tree!

ERICA: The black shirts beat him bloody.

BRIAN: This is a working instrument.

ERICA: I visited Arturo in hospital and played a Bach gavotte to raise his spirits.

BRIAN: Without even drawing a bow across the strings, I know…

ERICA: Arturo sat up and applauded. "Brava, signora Morini! Brava!"

BRIAN: …this will be clear and bold and bell-like all the way up the G-string.

ERICA: Arturo presented me with the silk scarf he was wearing.

(BRIAN *spots something on the C bout of the violin.*)

ERICA: Brava!

(BRIAN *and* ERICA *stop simultaneously.*)

BRIAN: *(To* ERICA*)* How did this happen?

ERICA: I don't wish to discuss it.

BRIAN: Somebody scraped it—right through the varnish all the way down to white wood. How could you let this happen?

ERICA: You think I can't care for a rare instrument? The Davidoff has been with me longer than you've been alive, Mister Skarstad! I could no more abuse it than you could abuse one of your children.

BRIAN: You realize if you give this to Pierre it will be all over town in five minutes.

ERICA: Which is precisely why I called you. I expect you to correct it with passion. And discretion.

BRIAN: I'll just play a quick chromatic scale…

ERICA: You'll do nothing of the sort. This is not the Nevada Youth Symphony.

BRIAN: Utah. I hate Nevada.

ERICA: So long as I'm alive, no one else will play the Davidoff.

BRIAN: How do you expect me to evaluate it?

ERICA: You shall hear me play. This very instrument.

(ERICA *crosses to a cabinet and removes an old record album. She places the L P on the spindle of a stereo record player and lowers the stylus onto the precise cut. BRIAN winces as she drags the needle across the vinyl. And again at the hiss and pop of pre-C D surface noise.*)

ERICA: My last public performance.

(We hear the Cadenza from Tchaikovsky's

Violin Concerto in D major.)

BRIAN: The Tchaikovsky. What else?

(The violin is resonant, strong, penetrating.)

ERICA: My signature piece.

BRIAN: Very muscular.

ERICA: The critics said I played like a man! They didn't think a woman was up to the Tchaikovsky. But I never wanted to be seen as a "woman" violinist. One hears good or bad, not man or woman. You are hearing?…

BRIAN: Some pretty slick Sevcik bowing, only better.

ERICA: I'm humbled by your praise.

BRIAN: Flawless, actually. Your playing is right there with the best.

ERICA: Not *the* best?

BRIAN: It is…virtuosic.

ERICA: That will do.

BRIAN: I'll just take it with me.

ERICA: Over my dead body!

BRIAN: I can't very well work on it here.

ERICA: I never leave this apartment and the Davidoff never leaves my sight.

BRIAN: If it's a question of security, your nurse...

ERICA: Dunham.

BRIAN: ...could open the lock on that cabinet with a hat pin.

ERICA: And probably has.

BRIAN: There are water marks on the door.

ERICA: A slight plumbing issue in the apartment above.

BRIAN: Do you know what water can do to glue joints, to varnish, to wood? It's not safe. Hell, you don't even trust your housekeeper with the tea service.

ERICA: She's the least of my concerns. There's the night doorman, the accountant, the neighbor, the nurse...

BRIAN: This isn't an apartment—it's a game of "Clue". Look, I've got a safe in my shop.

ERICA: The silver cabinet is safe enough.

BRIAN: If you're afraid to go outside...

ERICA: Afraid?

BRIAN: ...I'll take it to storage at Sotheby's.

ERICA: I don't want it stored. I want it restored to its former perfection.

(BRIAN *writes down his contact information on a paper napkin and hands it to* ERICA.)

BRIAN: Here's my address. Do I have your permission to leave?

ERICA: *(Beat)* On the condition you say nothing of this to anyone, I will personally deliver it to your workshop—that is, assuming you can repair the damage.

BRIAN: I will make it invisible.

ERICA: I shall expect no less. Now, dear boy, I'm tired. Make yourself invisible!

(BRIAN exits. ERICA lovingly lifts the Davidoff to her chin, raises the bow, turns up the Tchaikovsky recording and without touching bow to string remembers exactly what it was to play that piece.)

(In silhouette, a YOUNG WOMAN plays a portion of the first movement of the Tchaikovsky Violin Concerto in D. The music swells.)

Two

(A cramped workshop on the second floor of Brian's home. BRIAN wears his shop apron and is bent over his workbench. He cradles the Strad and painstakingly applies a coat of varnish with a tiny brush. ERICA sits to the side in a worn armchair. She holds a book but exhibits little interest in it. Time passes. It's night—the end of a long day. A dog barks outside.)

ERICA: The train from Boston was very fast that day. Making up for lost time, I suppose. Papa was waiting for me in New York. Another girl in the compartment was traveling alone. She was my age—fourteen. Her name was Dorothy. She was off to visit her grandmother. I told her I was going to play my very first concert at Carnegie Hall. She seemed to feel sorry for me. Isn't that silly? She asked if I would still play concerts once I had children? "I'll never have children. They take up too much time." She said she would name a daughter for me. *(Remembering the view)* Suddenly the view opened up. Through the window I saw the ocean. The salt marsh. The seagulls. It went by so quickly. *(Glances at her watch)* Oh, for heaven's sake, it's nearly nine thirty.

BRIAN: Huh?

ERICA: I mustn't miss the late train.

BRIAN: Yes, you told me that.

ERICA: Did I?

BRIAN: Fifteen minutes ago. And fifteen minutes before that. And fifteen minutes...what you were doing riding a train in the first place...you should have hired a car.

ERICA: I'm not made of money. And I'm never gone so long. It's bad enough the nurse has the run of the place. Before you know it she'll call the attorney and the attorney will call the conservator and the conservator will call a press conference...

BRIAN: Call the nurse. Feel free to use the phone.

ERICA: We have nothing to say to each other. The woman is a conversational black hole. To think my apartment was once filled with music, musicians. The times I had Jascha to dinner, Arturo, Lenny—you couldn't shut them up. Especially Lenny, when he was onto his favorite subject.

BRIAN: Which was?

ERICA: Lenny. Ugh, and that horrid little violin prodigy he used to drag around with him. Practically had the same name—what was it, Bornstein?

BRIAN: Eugene Bornstein? You knew Eugene Bornstein?

ERICA: Impostor. Upstart.

BRIAN: Superstar.

ERICA: Media whore! Except for me, the old crowd has gone the way of the dinosaurs! Is it any wonder I don't venture outside my apartment?

BRIAN: If this is your idea of "out".

(The dog continues to bark.)

ERICA: I'm asked all the time, mind you. Philharmonic Opening Night. The Met. Benefits, soirees. "Last Living legend of music," and all that. Only last week I was invited to conduct a master class at the Mannes School of Music. Naturally, I said "no," of course.

BRIAN: Why "no?"

ERICA: Such fuss and bother over nothing. As if I could transmit a lifetime of knowledge through mere osmosis. And I simply detest students. Anyway, it's the Davidoff they want to see, not me.

BRIAN: Somehow I doubt that.

ERICA: Really? And who was it couldn't wait to get out of my apartment until he opened that case?

BRIAN: I was uncomfortable—out of my element.

ERICA: What element is that?

BRIAN: *(Shouts out the open door)* Will somebody let the dog in?!

(The dog mercifully stops barking.)

BRIAN: Look, a building on Fifth Avenue with the Doorman From Hell. And that beady-eyed neighbor in the lobby. The woman he lives with must be twice his age. I heard him call her "mummy".

ERICA: Well, she did adopt him.

BRIAN: That element! And between you and me, "mummy's" made one too many visits to the plastic surgeon. I've seen livelier faces at Madame Tussaud's.

ERICA: You're saying I live in the waxworks? Like *Sunset Boulevard*?

BRIAN: I wouldn't go that far.

ERICA: *(As Norma Desmond)* "I'm still big. It's the music that got small!" Laugh. I'm having fun with you.

BRIAN: It's not always easy to tell. I'm glad I got you out.

ERICA: Did my watch stop?

BRIAN: You realize a restoration like this normally takes days?

ERICA: Normality is one vice I've always managed to avoid. Would you care for more strudel?

(ERICA *offers a plate to* BRIAN.)

BRIAN: I think I have maybe six kinds of toxic chemicals on my hands...

(ERICA *forces a bite of strudel into* BRIAN's *mouth. He cranes his neck and holds the violin far away from the flying crumbs.*)

BRIAN: Mmm, delicious.

ERICA: It will help you forget those cunning little white gelatinous cubes at dinner.

BRIAN: Tofu. My wife is into macrobiotics. This month.

ERICA: Ah, the happy homemaker.

BRIAN: I wouldn't say that.

ERICA: She isn't happy?

BRIAN: She isn't a homemaker. She's a composer. Well, aspiring. She studied with Ussachevsky.

ERICA: (*Mildly impressed*) Vladimir! Quite the ladies man, in his day. Vlad the Impaler, we called him!

BRIAN: He was nintey years old. On a walker. She's very talented. Her cello composition won a national contest.

ERICA: Funny that didn't come up over dinner.

BRIAN: It wouldn't. She's very modest. And you're kind of...

ERICA: Not?

BRIAN: Your resume can be a bit…

ERICA: Intimidating? And how might you have finally familiarized yourself with my intimidating past?

BRIAN: The Internet.

ERICA: I feel rather exposed.

BRIAN: "A sonority of tone."

ERICA: *The New York Times*—my Carnegie Hall debut! The critics liked to point out my tone. It wasn't always a compliment.

BRIAN: I guess they thought that for a woman…

ERICA: It wasn't ladylike? To hell with that! I always had a big tone. I'm an old-fashioned romantic. Ach, these young musicians today treat a violin like a porcelain figurine, as if it could burst into a thousand pieces at the merest touch. Where I come from the violin is first a folk instrument. No pampering. Play it loud over the noisy crowd. Pour yourself into every note and the notes will come back like a thunderclap, or a whisper. Play it like you mean it. *(Checks her watch)* Heavens—look at the time!

BRIAN: If you're that worried, my wife can run you back into the City.

ERICA: Without the Davidoff? Impossible. I might be persuaded to spend the night.

BRIAN: I don't think you'd much like the convertible sofa. Plus, I've got to run the boys to the orthodontist first thing. Braces, both of them—just what I need. And the dog is overdue for deworming. *(Briefly turning his back)*

ERICA: Such an abundant life. And here I am under foot. I'll bid adieu.

(ERICA picks up the instrument. BRIAN turns back in shock, pursuing her and taking the violin from her.)

BRIAN: What are you doing?! The varnish isn't dry! This is a critical stage of the process. You wouldn't snatch a patient from the operating table in the middle of surgery, would you?

ERICA: You don't have to bite my head off.

BRIAN: Mrs Morini, I'm sure performing in public was second nature to you. But I generally work alone. At my own pace. I don't see what all the hurry is about— and the secrecy.

ERICA: You must understand, to be a certain age is to accept that your life is no longer your own. At my age there are attorneys, conservators, accountants, executors and God knows what other vultures constantly circling.

BRIAN: You scraped the bow against the top, didn't you?

ERICA: No. Never.

BRIAN: It's not a crime. I see that sort of thing all the time. Especially with musicians who are, say, a little rusty.

ERICA: Rusty? I'm not a piece of machinery.

BRIAN: It was probably something else.

ERICA: If the conservator thought for even one second that I was incompetent…

BRIAN: He could take it away?

ERICA: *(Beat)* Not if I sell it first.

BRIAN: You want to sell the Davidoff?

ERICA: Would you rather I wait for one of the vultures to steal it? This is what I have to do.

BRIAN: And you think you can count on me to keep my mouth shut. Like it never happened.

ERICA: I have nothing further to say on the subject.

BRIAN: I'll just go back to work.

ERICA: I'll go back to my book. Sardou. In French. I'm getting a good deal of reading done.

BRIAN: *(Continuing the repair)* If I was short with you...I'm under some pressure here. Layer after layer of varnish. And time to dry. See each rare instrument has its own color and hue. I don't use dragon's blood varnish like those quick-fix restorers. I've got a golden-orange undercoat, perfect brown on top of that, then alizarin, maybe Cremonese red. And now you tell me it's going to be scrutinized...

ERICA: I've started this paragraph over three times.

BRIAN: I'm trying to explain so you'll know why when an appraiser looks at this—my work—he won't see my work. Only Strad's.

(Loud electric guitars squawk from the room below. ERICA puts down her book.)

ERICA: For God's sake, please stop that unbearable racket!

BRIAN: *(Stomps on the floor)* Hey, knock it off! No guitars until you're done practicing violin.

(The guitars stop. To ERICA as if to explain...)

BRIAN: Boys. *(He applies the final brush strokes the violin.)*

ERICA: Have I said something to upset you?

BRIAN: Everything you say upsets me.

ERICA: Something in particular?

BRIAN: I just finished an impossible restoration under impossible circumstances. And somebody else is going to have the benefit.

ERICA: You'll be fairly compensated for your work.

BRIAN: I'm not talking about money. Whoever sells this will have the benefit of knowing he helped sustain the

legacy of possibly the most perfect Strad in existence.
The fact that there was an imperfection I made go
away is a secret between you, me and Strad. I'm okay
with that. I don't know, maybe I'm tired of being such
a well-kept secret.

ERICA: Perhaps you would have had a more artistic
career without the distraction of "dogs" and "boys".

BRIAN: I generally avoid artists at all costs. Art is for
people who can afford it. The rest of us have to work
for a living.

ERICA: I haven't worked?!

BRIAN: I don't mean you.

ERICA: What other artists are there in this room? An
Artist is someone who is unwilling to compromise!
You think I haven't asked myself how life might have
been different with children? It was out of the question.
My manager would have dropped me in a heartbeat.
No matter—I had a gift! The gifted do not squander
their time. I wasn't some faux prodigy. I was the
genuine article.

BRIAN: Oh, and what is a *real* child prodigy?

ERICA: To not know how you do what you do, and to
do it anyway. To have a gift, and not be devoured by it.
To be a child, but never have a childhood.

BRIAN: Well, I've got children and I've got to…

ERICA: …provide for them?

(*Uninspired violin scales from the next room.*)

BRIAN: You like to complete my sentences, don't you?

ERICA: When I know where they're going. Brian—
where are you going?

(*The violin scales are punishingly bad.*)

BRIAN: *(Closes the shop door)* Pierre Bouchier offered me that job again.

ERICA: Ah, a first rate shop with a chandelier, and no dogs, or boys. You told him?

BRIAN: I'd sleep on it. You have to understand, this job would mean a steady income. Health insurance. The work would be nothing especially inspiring - mostly repairs, tune-ups.

ERICA: Instrument making?

BRIAN: That was not in the job description.

ERICA: If you were any kind of an artist you would have told him *Va te faire foutre! Parlez vous francais?*

BRIAN: Yeah. "Go fu——"

(The violins are horrendous.)

BRIAN: They do it to spite me.

(BRIAN stomps on the floor. The violins stop.)

BRIAN: Done. *(He removes the Strad from under the lamp.)* And done.

(ERICA takes it, turns it over in the light.)

ERICA: Passable enough, to the naked eye.

BRIAN: *Passible? I* can't see it anymore. Have a better look.

(ERICA inspects it with a magnifying glass.)

ERICA: It's invisible.

BRIAN: I told you it would be. Let me show you something.

(BRIAN hands ERICA a quarter cut plank of maple.)

ERICA: What's that?

BRIAN: *(Taps his finger on the plank)* A violin. Or it will be when I get around to it.

ERICA: Looks like a piece of wood.

BRIAN: And sheet music looks like paper until *you* remove a concerto from it. I just remove wood until all that's left is a violin. Paper, maple—we both start with a tree. *(Takes back the maple)* Now that we know we come from the same place, you think you might tell me how the Davidoff was damaged?

ERICA: *(Beat)* There was a time when I was mentioned in the same breath as Kreisler, Elman, Heifetz! I memorized Paganini's Caprice #24 in one reading! Now I give violin lessons to a select few hopeless students whose pushy parents are certain they have spawned prodigies. This one young woman was making such a hash of Bruch I could bear it no longer. "Here," I told her, "I'll show you." I never even felt the ebony of the bow against the spruce top. But when I looked down at white wood...

BRIAN: What white wood?

ERICA: What, indeed.

BRIAN: So I guess you'll list it with Sotheby's.

ERICA: Sotheby's is a brothel. I could no more auction off the Davidoff than auction off my soul. You're not very good at business, even if you are a fine...

BRIAN: Repairman?

ERICA: I'll thank you not to finish *my* sentence. That master class at the Mannes School?

BRIAN: I thought you didn't have time for that kind of thing.

ERICA: Time, I'm afraid, is a commodity that is in ever shorter supply.

BRIAN: You don't have to talk about it if...

ERICA: I'm not in my death throes, thank you. I have an incurable condition known as "old age". As it belatedly occurs to me that I might not live forever, I have to accept certain responsibilities. You might wish to be present at Mannes for the last time I appear in public with the Davidoff.

BRIAN: Kind of a farewell to the troops?

ERICA: And a little free advertising never hurt.

BRIAN: So you plan to sell it without Sotheby's. I'm sure Pierre will be thrilled to cash in.

ERICA: Do you really think I would entrust the Davidoff to that old pirate? No, I would like you to sell it for me.

BRIAN: *(Stunned)* You're not serious?

ERICA: I'm indeed most serious. It will make you a man of means. I imagine it's worth three million dollars.

BRIAN: Three and a half, conservatively. At standard commission of twenty percent, that's...seven hundred thousand dollars!

ERICA: I was thinking of something more like fifteen percent.

BRIAN: That's still a miracle.

(BRIAN *starts to hug* ERICA. *She recoils.)*

ERICA: I have a low threshold for gratitude.

BRIAN: How can I properly thank you?

ERICA: You can start by driving me home. With all your jabbering, it's gotten ungodly late. Perhaps we can stop along the way for some marmalade.

Variation

*(A recital hall at the Mannes School of Music. ERICA sits
in an arm chair, as regal as a queen on her throne. BRIAN
watches from the wings. ERICA speaks into a microphone on
a stand.)*

ERICA: No, no, no no no. Beautiful.

(The music stops.)

ERICA: That was perfect. So why do I stop you?
Your bow and finger technique are perfect. But real
technique is a matter of the heart and mind, not
the fingers. Such a face—I have disconcerted you. I
will let you in on a little secret -violinists are utterly
replaceable. In the symphony orchestra you are a
sprocket in a large machine. In a quartet, the machine
is merely smaller. The few of you who become
soloists are told you are unique. Don't believe it.
You are a fashion that comes and goes. Now you are
all depressed. *(Adjusts the microphone)* When I was
younger than the youngest of you here, I made my
New York debut at Carnegie Hall. Do you know what
it is to perform on the stage of the greatest concert hall
in America at an age when most children are more
worried about pimples? Can you grasp the sacrifice
that is required? When you step into that light, you
might never again step back out of it. Yes, they say
the way to get to Carnegie Hall is practice, practice,
practice. No. Practice is not enough. You do not play
the violin. You must *become* the violin! After my debut,
I was presented with the Maud Powell Guadagnini,
which she had bequeathed to "the next great woman
violinist". When one is young one hears only the word
"great". When one is less young one hears only the
word "next". There is always the next, and the next,
and the next. I did not perform on the Guadagnini. For
me, there was only ever one violin.

(BRIAN *hands* ERICA *the Davidoff. She holds it up for all to see.*)

ERICA: The Karl Davidoff Stradivarius. Named for it's previous owner, a cellist of all things. *(Cradles the Davidoff)* It has been a long and beautiful union. But be forewarned—while music and musical instruments are immortal, we musicians sadly are not. Lately, I have only to cross the room to be reminded of my own mortality.

So I let you in on another secret. Life is a symphony. A composition in four movements: allegro, adagio, scherzo, allegro. Fast, slow, lively, faster. The fastness of it all takes my breath away. I find myself amidst the final movement of my life, and it is rather shocking. I know now it is the third movement you must savor. This is the scherzo, the dance. For if we fully embrace life and we are true to our own art, then each of us is unique. Never compromise. Hold nothing back. Play it like you mean it! So in the end you can say, "I played life's symphony bold and true." Thank you.

(ERICA *regally acknowledges the applause.*)

Three

(ERICA's *apartment. She wears a simple black dress she might have once worn to perform.* BRIAN *wears a rumpled blue blazer and tie over faded jeans. He closes the door on unseen visitors. The Davidoff is in its case on the coffee table.*)

BRIAN: We can't thank you enough for stopping by. Safe back. *(He closes the door. A beat. He breaks out in laughter.)*

ERICA: Shhh. They'll hear.

BRIAN: I watched them all the way into the elevator.

ERICA: *(Laughs)* I've never seen such an unrelenting smile.

BRIAN: She was Miss Oklahoma, 1987.

ERICA: Imagine the facial muscles it takes to maintain a smile like that.

BRIAN: I read somewhere they put Vaseline on their teeth. It keeps the lips from drying out during the smiling. She's an epic smiler. She finished first in the talent competition at the Miss America pageant.

ERICA: She has ghastly technique.

BRIAN: You might ask her husband about that.

ERICA: Husband? I thought he was her grandfather!

BRIAN: Oil money makes the years just melt away.

ERICA: That and whatever use she might make of all that Vaseline in her mouth.

BRIAN: Signora Morini!

ERICA: You think that sort of thing doesn't go on in the classical music world?

BRIAN: It does?

ERICA: Hardly ever. Most musicians would prefer "bravo" over fellatio any day. *(Shudders)*

BRIAN: "Bravo!"

ERICA: How you ever talked me into letting that woman touch the Davidoff let alone play it…

BRIAN: Maybe I could give it a whirl.

ERICA: Don't push your luck.

BRIAN: I don't know about you, but I've never heard a finer rendition of "America the Beautiful." Okay, I admit it, she really sucks—pardon the choice of words. But you've been pretty liberal with your veto power all week. And it's good for the remaining customers to know there's competition. It will be better with Bornstein.

ERICA: You mean that Liberace is coming here today?

BRIAN: *(Pointing)* His name is on the appointment list. Right after Miss Oklahoma.

ERICA: Finally in his proper place.

BRIAN: Come on. It's hard to fault his credentials. One of the youngest Juilliard graduates ever. Five Grammy awards.

ERICA: Are you sure they weren't "hammy" awards. Those absurd facial expressions. *(Imitates faux ecstasy)* Overcome by his own emotions. What a load of crap. The man is up there having sex with himself.

BRIAN: Where did you see him play?

ERICA: I believe it was on a P B S fundraiser. In front of a fountain. At Disney World.

BRIAN: Alright, alright. Well he seemed very interested when we spoke. So what if he's a diva?

ERICA: Oh, he's not even worthy of the designation. The man is a technician. A diva must be tempestuous, passionate. As passion-arousing instruments go, I'm given to believe Mister B's is rather *diminuendo.*

BRIAN: His audience is rather "humongumendo".

ERICA: A pack of Philistines who applaud between movements and listen to Barry Manilow on the way home. I don't want to talk about Bornstein.

BRIAN: Would you mind if we talked about money for a minute?

ERICA: I ordinarily leave that to my accountant.

BRIAN: The thing is I already talked to my tax guy. He said I'd take a smaller hit if the commission came incrementally instead of in one lump sum. Now he thinks it's possible to structure this in a way...

ERICA: Relax. It's only money.

BRIAN: Money is never only money. I mean, fifteen percent of three-point-five million comes to five hundred and twenty-five thousand dollars. That's years of work for me. Money for the boys' college. Money to repair the running toilet, the leaky storm windows, the rotting gutters. Money to pay off the mortgage—mortgages. To buy an engagement ring for my wife. Oh, and a private studio for her with a brand new Steinway baby grand. And matching Stratocasters for the boys.

ERICA: Strad-o?...

BRIAN: Stratocasters. Electrified stringed instruments.

ERICA: Guitars.

BRIAN: Strats, in rock parlance.

ERICA: And what is so special about a Strat?

BRIAN: It has three pick-ups instead of one. And the Whammy Bar, I mean, you could light a cigarette, read a magazine, the note would still be playing.

ERICA: The bowing I had to do. If only I'd plugged in.

BRIAN: All the greats had Stratocasters—Clapton, Hendrix, Lennon...

ERICA: When he wasn't murdering the Czar.

BRIAN: John Lennon.

ERICA: I know. I'm not that much of a dinosaur. In any case, I preferred the Rolling Stones. Michael Jagger visited me backstage at Town Hall and said he was an enormous fan. *(Beat)* Strats, Steinways - all this virtuous selfless purchasing for others. You would want nothing for yourself?

BRIAN: *(Thinks)* Time. Time to lock the door to the shop. Unplug the phone. Time to do the work I want to do.

ERICA: Original Skarstads!

BRIAN: Yeah, but, let's face it, there's not what you would call a great demand for them.

ERICA: Time will tell. Aren't you going to ask me what I'd do with my share of the proceeds?

BRIAN: Is it any of my business?

ERICA: No, but we've already exhausted the subject of oral sex. *(Beat)* I will leave everything to Hadassah.

BRIAN: Hadassah?

ERICA: You find that amusing?

BRIAN: I just don't think of Italians endowing Jewish organizations.

ERICA: Historically Italians are great philanthropists and patrons of the arts. I just don't happen to be Italian.

BRIAN: "Morini" is an Italian name.

ERICA: Of course it is. It's just not my name. It was all father's doing. "The Great violinists are Italian." Naturally, he took an Italian name.

BRIAN: Instead of?…

ERICA: Morgenstern.

BRIAN: He must have noticed that the great violinists of the twentieth century tended less to be Italian than…

ERICA: Jewish? Father was not known for his foresight. Oh, what does it matter? Music is my religion.

BRIAN: Then how did you end up marrying a Sicilian diamond broker?

ERICA: It's enough to perform with musicians. You don't have to date them, too.

BRIAN: You dated?

ERICA: You find that so hard to believe?

BRIAN: I didn't know that's how it was done.

ERICA: Back in the Dark Ages?

BRIAN: In Vienna.

ERICA: I'll have you know I had more than my share of beaus. I was quite a dancer in my day.

BRIAN: I'm sure…

ERICA: But when one starts concertizing at such an early age there are certain, what's the word…?

BRIAN: Sacrifices?

ERICA: Gaps is a better word. One can always fill in gaps.

BRIAN: You know, I'm going to confirm with Bornstein.

ERICA: What is your hurry? Remember the symphony of life?

BRIAN: My life is no symphony.

ERICA: Certainly it is. You're too caught up in the moment to see. The third movement is the most important, dear. The third movement, the scherzo, the dance, minuet.

(ERICA *fumbles with the record player.* BRIAN *can't stand to hear her scratch another record.*)

BRIAN: I've got it.

(*We hear a Mozart minuet.*)

BRIAN: Mozart. I played this when I was a kid.

ERICA: Slow down a little. Dance.

BRIAN: Metaphorically speaking.

ERICA: There is a lady present, not a metaphor.

BRIAN: My minuet-ing is a little…

ERICA: …rusty?

BRIAN: Non-existent is probably the word I was looking for.

ERICA: No one's watching. I've given Nurse Dunham the afternoon off. One could fake it. Or not.

(ERICA *reaches for the record player but* BRIAN *intercepts her hand. He's not sure what to do next.*)

ERICA: Yes?

BRIAN: May I have this dance, Madame Morini?

ERICA: Do call me Erica.

(ERICA *is very ladylike as she does something resembling a minuet.* BRIAN *is game but little more as he tries to follow. He gets better as the dance goes on.*)

(*The minuet transforms from scratchy recorded music to live music played by the* YOUNG WOMAN *in silhouette.*)

(ERICA *seems caught up in some romantic dream. The dance becomes uncomfortably intimate for* BRIAN. *He breaks away and stops the record. The* YOUNG WOMAN *disappears.*)

BRIAN: We should probably get back to business.

ERICA: All work and no play…

BRIAN: I'm not here to play. I'm here to make a sale. Not that we're making much progress that way. Maybe we could move up Bornstein's appointment. You know, word on the street is he's really ready to buy. He wants to add the Davidoff to his personal collection.

(BRIAN *dials the number.* ERICA's *expression suddenly sours.*)

ERICA: The Davidoff will not be part of a "collection." It's not a museum piece. It must be played. (*She reaches for the phone.*) Allow me. (*She speaks into the phone.*) Hello, Eugene. Madame Morini here. Yes, I'm aware you are planning to visit. I just wanted to say you needn't bother. No, I'm feeling fine. I simply don't feel you are up to owning the Davidoff. If you must know, the truth is you are a conservatory brat and a pitiful hack who wouldn't know the correct pitch if it crawled up your backside. You shouldn't be let near a rare instrument. Well, you don't have to get huffy. I beg your pardon? *(She hangs up the phone.)*

ERICA: There are plenty of other fish in the symphony.

BRIAN: What did you just do?

ERICA: The man is a pig.

BRIAN: A pig worth millions.

ERICA: Do you know what he said to me?

BRIAN: I heard what you said to him.

ERICA: He said the Davidoff and I deserve each other because neither of us was much to look at anymore.

BRIAN: So he's an asshole. But he's our best customer. I'll call him back. Tell him you're having a bad day. *(He reaches for the phone.)*

ERICA: Touch that phone and our arrangement is off!

BRIAN: Whoa. If you feel that strongly about it. Okay, I picked the wrong guy. We'll start fresh tomorrow.

ERICA: It's not just Bornstein. It's everybody. I'm not selling.

BRIAN: Not selling today?

ERICA: Not ever. I changed my mind.

BRIAN: When? When did you change your mind?

ERICA: I had second thoughts from the start.

BRIAN: If I said something, did something…

ERICA: It wasn't any one thing. But when we danced…

BRIAN: I warned you I was a lousy dancer.

ERICA: Why were you even dancing with me?

BRIAN: It seemed like the gentlemanly…

ERICA: Why was Bornstein coming here today?

BRIAN: This is a trick question.

ERICA: This is *the* question! Why has anyone ever shown the least interest in me?

BRIAN: You're kind of fun in your way.

ERICA: Fun? Am I doing card tricks? Making balloon animals? I am not now nor have I ever been fun. Do not insult me with flattery. The truth is that people put up with me, pretend to like me, because of my talent. Well, that's long gone. All I have left is the Davidoff. And if that's gone I might as well vanish into thin air.

BRIAN: Be realistic—you can't take it to the grave with you.

ERICA: Maybe I will!

BRIAN: This is clearly a bad time. I'll come back in the morning.

ERICA: And will you come back at all if I tell you it will be no different tomorrow? Will you join me for tea, ask me to dance if I say there will be no sale?

BRIAN: I like you Erica. I'm sorry you don't have a better opinion of yourself. But I really don't have the patience for this right now. Because all of this is costing me time and money.

ERICA: There. That's all I am to you—a payday.

BRIAN: What pay? I'm out gas, tolls, marmalade, and I haven't seen the first dollar. I could get more for babysitting.

ERICA: Instead of babysitting an arthritic old crone?

BRIAN: Don't be ridiculous.

ERICA: But I am ridiculous. What's more ridiculous than a child prodigy who outlives her childhood? I gave up everything for music. I will not give up the Davidoff. I'm sorry if I've disappointed you.

BRIAN: Disappointed? No. Ambushed, I think, says it better. Obliterated. You let me build up this fragile dream and then, BOOM! Why the hell did you call me in the first place?

ERICA: I had reason to believe you would make the damage invisible.

BRIAN: Why not call Pierre Bouchier? Why call me?

ERICA: Because *you* are invisible. Who knew you were also a vulture, just like the rest of them?

BRIAN: Now you're being paranoid.

ERICA: You hate me. Say it.

BRIAN: Let's not say anything we'll regret.

ERICA: Say it. Mercenary.

BRIAN: That's not funny.

ERICA: Carpenter.

BRIAN: Okay, that's enough.

ERICA: Repairman.

BRIAN: I'm out of here.

ERICA: That's right, run, the way you run from your gift. Do menial labor for Pierre.

BRIAN: Don't push me.

ERICA: Pushing people is what I do. I'm difficult.

BRIAN: Difficult? You're impossible!

ERICA: I'm insufferable. But I've earned the right to be. What have you earned, you hack!?

BRIAN: The right to tell you to shut up!

ERICA: I will not shut up.

BRIAN: For once in your precious, spoiled, narcissistic life, shut the hell up!

ERICA: I will not shut up.

BRIAN: Oh yes you will. One way or another. You know, you might be the greatest woman violinist who ever lived, but as far as I can tell you stopped living a long time ago. So you're an artiste. Well, I hope your art curls up in your lap and kisses you "goodnight" at bed time. I hope it comforts you in your old age. I hope your art comes to weep at your grave. But if you ask me, art is a poor substitute for love. *(Crosses to the door)* You know, for a few minutes here today, you really were fun. Almost likable. Now? Yeah, you're just a payday. And a pretty lousy one at that. *(Exits)*

(ERICA is suddenly short of breath. She lowers herself onto the settee.)

Four

(Late night, Admitting at Mount Sinai Hospital. ERICA is seated in a wheel-chair. BRIAN rushes in and finds her.)

BRIAN: I came as soon as I heard.

ERICA: I'm not sick.

BRIAN: The phone rang and I…

ERICA: I'm not sick!

BRIAN: …was already awake. As if I…

ERICA: I'm not sick!

BRIAN: …knew a call was coming. How are you?

ERICA: I'm not sick.

BRIAN: Then why are you being admitted to a hospital?

ERICA: I'm not sick.

BRIAN: You're feeling fine?

ERICA: I'm not unwell. A spell, is all. I will go now. *(Tries to stand)*

BRIAN: I don't think that's how it works.

(BRIAN sits ERICA back down in the wheelchair.)

BRIAN: They'll want to run tests, do all that hospital stuff.

ERICA: It's simply some nonsense with my heart.

BRIAN: What the doctor said on the phone...do you want to know?

ERICA: I've no patience for medical mumbo jumbo.

BRIAN: You're here because fluid has been building up in your body for some time.

ERICA: I'm here because Nurse Dunham wanted me out of the house so the vultures can have the run of the place.

BRIAN: That's a little far-fetched.

ERICA: I know what I'm talking about. I am not mentally incompetent. So if you're thinking of going over to their side...

BRIAN: Whose side?

ERICA: The vultures—they're offering to cut you in, I suppose. What do you care what happens to the Davidoff? You just want to take your commission and run!

BRIAN: I'm here. I'm not running anywhere.

ERICA: Not yet. But I've got my eye on you. Take, take, take. That's all these people know. Do they ever give me what I want? Did you bring me anything?

BRIAN: It's 3 A M. This is my pajama top.

ERICA: That would explain the little bears. I thought you would bring me something.

BRIAN: *I'm* here. The doctor called me. I came.

ERICA: To insult me more?

BRIAN: I was hoping you'd forget that.

ERICA: I never forget a bad review.

BRIAN: There's a kind of non-remembering that's not so much forgetting as it is good manners. I shouldn't have said the things I said.

ERICA: You may think of me as some armor-plated Valkyrie. But I'm a frail old woman. I bruise easily.

BRIAN: I can be a little self-righteous when I've been wronged.

ERICA: You think?

BRIAN: That's no excuse. I apologize.

ERICA: Accepted. Possibly I said some things, myself.

BRIAN: Nothing really comes to mind.

ERICA: Please, spare me your good manners. I say the most awful things to people. I hear myself saying them and think only an awful person would say that. Am I awful?

BRIAN: We both speak our minds.

ERICA: Not always. Not now, thank you. Thank you for not mentioning the breathing.

BRIAN: I'm all for it. Breathing.

ERICA: How shallow it is. The pulmonologist insists I stay for observation. Like some prisoner. As a child I hated being kept inside for mere sniffles. I would bang around my room, "I'm not sick. I'm not sick!" I'm going.

(Starts to stand again.)

BRIAN: This is more than sniffles.

ERICA: Papa couldn't keep me inside. Do you think you can?

BRIAN: I'm not going to fight you, Erica.

(ERICA *relents and sits back down.*)

ERICA: I'm not sick. What I am is very, very spoiled.

BRIAN: You're an artist.

ERICA: Artists are children. That's why they shouldn't have them. But my husband is gone. My art is gone. All I have left is the Davidoff.

BRIAN: It's a wooden box.

ERICA: So is a house. So is a coffin. It's the life inside that counts. You held it. I saw the expression on your face.

BRIAN: You want to know the truth? When I first saw that instrument it pissed me off! Here was something that was created almost three hundred years ago that I would never do, never even approach. But when the Davidoff was in my shop, on my bench, I held it and felt...forget it.

ERICA: You felt for one moment as if you knew what was in the mind of Stradivarius. You felt that his hands and yours were one

BRIAN: It's absurd.

ERICA: No, I've felt it, too. All artists feel it at some point.

BRIAN: I'm no artist. I'm a carpenter.

ERICA: We both know that's untrue. Violin makers make music by making instruments. Not, I must add, by repairing them.

BRIAN: I have to admit—I love the box!

ERICA: I've called my attorney. I must make plans. I will tell you on the way home.

(ERICA *tries to stand again. She is unsteady, lightheaded.* BRIAN *seems to embrace her as he lowers her back into the wheelchair.*)

BRIAN: Another "spell"?

(ERICA *nods.*)

BRIAN: It's probably nothing. But why not spend the night just to be on the safe side? Do it for me.

ERICA: You will do something for me. I need to know the Davidoff is safe.

BRIAN: You should be focusing on yourself, not the violin.

ERICA: You think there's a difference?

BRIAN: I'm sure it's okay.

ERICA: I need to hear it from you. Take my keys. Go there. Now. Be my eyes. I know I can count on you. You weren't the only one the doctor called. You're the only one who came. Do this for me. (*She removes the keys on the strand around her neck.*) I will not rest until I know it is safe. You'll go?

BRIAN: What else do I have to do at three in the morning?

ERICA: I'll wait for you. Go now! I'm not sick.

(BRIAN *takes the keys and exits.*)

ERICA: I'm not sick.

Variation

(BRIAN *enters* ERICA's *apartment. The place is eerily
filled with her presence. He can smell her perfume. She is
simultaneously in view in her hospital room. He turns on
a lamp light and crosses to the silver closet. He removes the
skeleton key from his pocket. He unlocks the silver cabinet.
He opens the violin case and removes the Toscanini scarf.)*

(A blinding light. BRIAN *answers questions from an unseen
interrogator.)*

BRIAN: I'm trying to explain. Eri…Mrs Morini gave me
the key.
She insisted I check on the Davidoff.
Yes, I did have the instrument in my home one time.
That's where my workshop is. It was in my home, and
so was she.
My job? I'm a violin restore(r)…maker.
Look, Mrs Morini asked me to sell the Davidoff but,
she changed her mind.
Who doesn't need money? I need money! You know,
I'm not the only one with access to her apartment - no,
officer, I'm not telling you how to do your job.
I know I'm in no position to ask a favor, but please…
Don't tell her it's been stolen.
She should hear it from someone she knows.

Coda

(ERICA's *hospital room. She lies propped up in hospital bed.*
BRIAN *enters and moves tentatively to her side, unsure if
she's awake.)*

BRIAN: Erica? Erica, there's something I need to tell…

ERICA: You didn't come back last night.

BRIAN: I thought we could both use the sleep.

ERICA: The Davidoff?

(BRIAN *removes the Toscanini scarf from his jacket pocket. Her face lights up.*)

ERICA: Thank God.

BRIAN: But Erica...

ERICA: All night I was on a train from Boston with Dorothy.

BRIAN: Dorothy?

ERICA: Is your memory failing? On my way to play Carnegie.

BRIAN: Oh, right, the woman in the train compartment.

ERICA: She was hardly a woman. Neither of us.

BRIAN: She was going to name a child for you.

ERICA: Children have a way of growing up. Growing old. You had something to tell me?

BRIAN: It completely slipped my mind.

(*We hear ambient hospital noise from the corridor.*)

ERICA: How do they expect anyone to think straight with that God awful noise?

BRIAN: You mean the heart monitor?

ERICA: A flat over C. Quarter notes. Eighths. Sixteenths. I can't bear that infernal racket. My thoughts are all pizzicato, pinging every which way. Carnegie Hall is so noisy!

BRIAN: Shhh. You're safe in a hospital room.

(BRIAN *helps* ERICA *take a sip of water. The coughing subsides. She remembers where she is.*)

ERICA: I'm drowning, you know.

BRIAN: You really shouldn't be talking.

ERICA: My lungs are filling up with fluid. I'm drowning in myself.

BRIAN: The doctors will fix it.

ERICA: The doctors stopped coming. They do that when they don't know what else to do. God complex. Poor losers.

BRIAN: The nurses here are very good.

ERICA: The nurses want to make me comfortable. I don't want to be comfortable. I want to play, feel the strings under my fingers, hear the notes fill the air.

BRIAN: Music, that's what you need. Maybe I can borrow a radio.

ERICA: Brian, I know what we have to do with the Davidoff.

BRIAN: Erica, the thing is…

ERICA: When I get out of here I will stipulate that only you can sell it. But you must promise that it will never be in a collection. The Davidoff will always be played.

(BRIAN *doesn't have the heart to tell her the truth.*)

BRIAN: You have my word.

ERICA: It must be a child. A girl. She should have imaginary friends, tea parties, feuds. She should climb a tree. But not too high. Not so high she tumbles and scrapes her perfect fingers on the way down. Life will fill the Davidoff. She will have a big tone. She will play it like she means it.

BRIAN: She'll call it the Morini Strad.

ERICA: Do you think so?

BRIAN: I do.

ERICA: I do, too. *(She has a pain in her chest.)*

BRIAN: I'll ring the nurse's station.

ERICA: No. They don't have what I want. Did you bring me anything?

BRIAN: You have to ask?

(*Pulls a jar of marmalade out of his coat.*)

ERICA: Good boy.

BRIAN: Grand Marnier! Would you like a taste?

ERICA: I have no appetite. A speck, perhaps.

(BRIAN *removes the lid. He looks around for a spoon, any utensil. Seeing none, he dips his baby finger into the marmalade and touches it to* ERICA's *lips.*)

ERICA: Take the rest to your wife. Is it macrobiotic?

BRIAN: She moved on to gluten-free. She's giving piano lessons to help out with the bills.

ERICA: What about composing?

BRIAN: Turns out she's been doing it all along. Gets up in the middle of the night. I thought it was my snoring.

ERICA: She can compose full time once you get your commission.

BRIAN: We're both very grateful to you. She's working on a violin piece in your honor.

ERICA: I am indeed honored. And Pierre Bouchier?

BRIAN: He called again with a job offer.

ERICA: You said "no?"

BRIAN: Words to that effect.

ERICA: I must know the exact words.

BRIAN: *Va te faire foutre!*

ERICA: *Tres bien!* Dearest Brian—Haruki said it plays like his Stradivarius.

BRIAN: What does?

ERICA: His Skarstad, of course.

BRIAN: He never said that. Not to me.

ERICA: Musicians say things to each other that are not meant for the ears of civilians.

BRIAN: I'm not a "civilian." I'm the guy who made the damn thing. He really said that?

ERICA: I heard him play it in recital. He was wrong. It does not play like his Stradivarius—it plays better!

BRIAN: That's why you chose me?

ERICA: You're tolerable to be around. And you've excellent taste in marmalade.

BRIAN: It wouldn't have anything to do with giving me a chance?

ERICA: A chance to do what?

BRIAN: Stop restoring. A chance to get back to making violins.

ERICA: I'm not that generous. I'm a diva. I only think of myself. Do we understand each other?

BRIAN: Yes, we do.

ERICA: *(Suddenly agitated)* Where is my scarf? My Toscanini scarf, man!

(BRIAN finds the Toscanini scarf and drapes it over her shoulders.)

BRIAN: Here.

(It fails to calm ERICA.)

ERICA: Good God, the noise!

(We enter ERICA's subjective soundscape—the ambient hospital sounds morph into the murmur of an audience as musicians tune up before a symphony performance.)

ERICA: The orchestra is tuning. My mind is blank. Where are the notes? Look at my hands. *(Her hands tremble.)* I can't catch my breath. *(She gasps.)* I'm afraid.

(BRIAN *takes* ERICA'*s hand.*)

(*Upstage transforms into a musician's eye view of Carnegie Hall. Tiers and boxes shimmer in the dim light.*)

(*The* YOUNG WOMAN *violinist steps into the light and plays the opening notes of the Tchaikovsky Violin Concerto in D—plays it like she means it! This calms* ERICA.)

ERICA: My breath. (*Her hands stop trembling.*) My hands. (*She places one hand over her heart.*) The notes are all here. (*Beat*) I have a confession to make—I lied.

BRIAN: Lied?

ERICA: About my age. Prodigies do.

BRIAN: So you're?...

ERICA: One year older. Do you mind?

BRIAN: I don't mind.

ERICA: Thank you.

(*The* YOUNG WOMAN *slowly disappears in light.*)

Epilogue

BRIAN: When I got out of college I took a job moving pianos to help pay off my student loans. Once we picked up a neglected old junker that people had just lost track of, and we took it to the town dump. We could have pushed it off the back of the truck, but for some reason we carried it down and placed it on the ground. Then we waited for the front loader to pull around and demolish it. You can't imagine the sound. Every string, every note that piano ever played, let go all at once in a singular anguished chord.
Erica was gone. She never knew the Davidoff was gone before her. You think I took it? What about the nurse, the neighbor, the conservator? As I told the investigating officer, "Would I live like this if I had a

three-and-a-half million dollar violin?" Hell, I feel like
it was stolen from *me*! That was *my* ticket out. That was
my future. Call me paranoid, but there are times when
I think Erica knew what happened to the Davidoff.
There are times when I think she engineered the whole
theft herself. Honest to God, as I stood over her casket
at Cedar Park, I pictured the damn thing in there under
her folded arms. Maybe you *can* take it with you!
Then this other image comes to me. A young girl
in Vienna, or Shanghai, or Brooklyn, arrives home
from school one day and opens a mysterious package
addressed in an unsteady hand. She pulls the twine,
peels back the brown paper, lifts the lid and beholds
the Davidoff. She gently cradles it under her chin
and is filled with the spirit of every note that has ever
flowed from its very fiber. She draws the bow across
the strings and the solitary plaintive notes ring out,
soulfully rippling outward until they reach a gnarled
elm tree in Cedar Park. The young girl smiles and
carefully puts the Davidoff aside to jump rope.
I was wrong when I told Erica that art is a poor
substitute for love. Art is… (*He is back in his workshop.*)
I came home from the funeral and caught the boys
practicing violin, of all things. I took the fiddles away
and handed them their old beat-up electric guitars,
"play it like you mean it!" (*He puts on his shop apron and
wearily stares at the high-paying neck graft restoration on
his bench. Before he quite knows what he's doing, he changes
his mind and takes out a piece of old golden brown quarter-
cut flamed maple and a large joiner plane.*) I will remove
wood until all that's left is a violin.

(*A* YOUNG WOMAN *in silhouette plays a majestic passage
from Tchaikovsky's Violin Concerto in D major. Black out*)

END OF PLAY